GOING TO THE
RAINFOREST

Rainforests are teeming with life — they are home to more than half of the world's animals. These **MACAWS** are native to the forests of Central and South America. Rainforests have very high yearly rainfall. They are usually very warm and wet places.

ORANGUTANS live in the oldest rainforests in the world on the South-East Asian islands of Borneo and Sumatra. The Indonesian name 'orang hutan' literally means 'people of the forest.' Orangutans spend more time in the trees than any of the other great apes.

6

The **EMPEROR TAMARIN** lives in groups in the rainforests of South America. This one is just a baby. Adult Emperor Tamarins have a long white moustache.

8

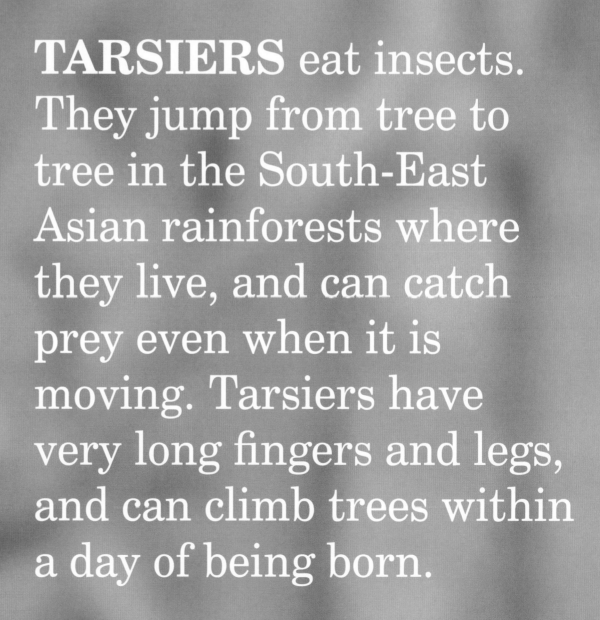

TARSIERS eat insects. They jump from tree to tree in the South-East Asian rainforests where they live, and can catch prey even when it is moving. Tarsiers have very long fingers and legs, and can climb trees within a day of being born.

THREE-TOED SLOTHS
live in the rainforests of
Central and South America.
They spend almost all their
time in trees. Their large
curved claws help them
grip branches.

LEMURS are native to the island of Madagascar, and live both in rainforests and dry inland areas. There are many different types of lemur — some can leap up to thirty feet from tree to tree. They will land upright with both their hands and feet gripping the tree branch.

The **SOUTHERN CASSOWARY** belongs to an ancient family of flightless birds that includes the Emu and the Ostrich. They search for fruit and fungi on the rainforest floor. Much of their natural habitat has been cleared, and there are now only about 1,500 living in the wild.

Cassowaries can be dangerous as they have a long, sharp spike on their inner toe.

TOUCANS roost together in holes in trees, which can become very cramped. To save space, toucans will tuck their bills and tails under their bodies.

Toucan wings are small, as they only need to fly short distances between the trees in the Central and South American rainforests where they live.

The **RED-EYED TREE FROG** lives in the tropical rainforests of Central and South America. It flashes its bright red eyes to startle predators such as birds or snakes.

MONKEY FROGS live in the rainforests of South America. Their long fingers allow them to grasp branches and to climb trees in the same way that monkeys climb.

21

IGUANAS are found in tropical areas of Central and South America and the Caribbean.

Iguanas have excellent eyesight, which they use to navigate through the crowded rainforests.

GREEN PYTHONS are found in Australia and New Guinea and spend most of their time curled around tree branches. They are well-camouflaged among the rainforest leaves.

These snakes are not venomous, but they do have very long front teeth, which they use to hold their prey.

SUMATRAN TIGERS
are native to the Indonesian island of Sumatra. Tiger stripes allow them to blend into the shadows of the trees as they sneak up on their prey.

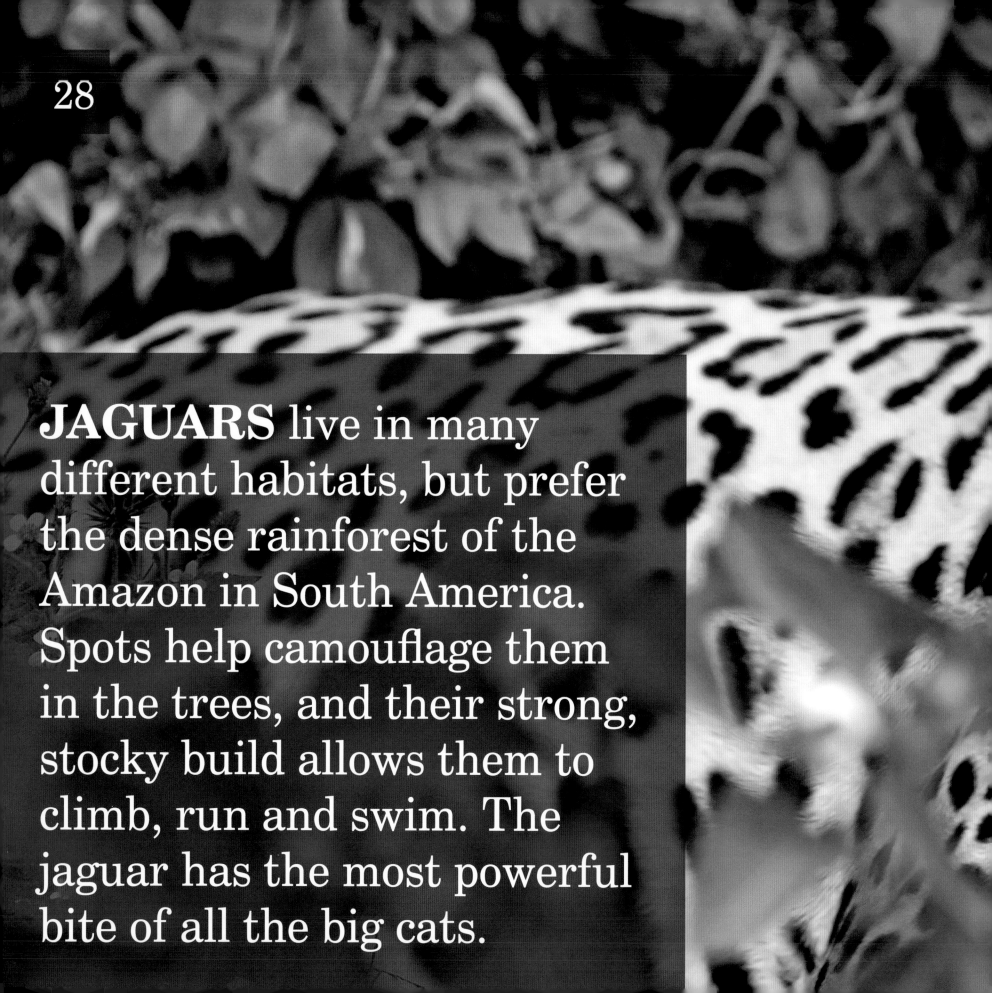

JAGUARS live in many different habitats, but prefer the dense rainforest of the Amazon in South America. Spots help camouflage them in the trees, and their strong, stocky build allows them to climb, run and swim. The jaguar has the most powerful bite of all the big cats.

The **BLUE MORPHO BUTTERFLY** lives in Central and South America and usually feeds on rotting fruit. Males live near the ground, and females live in the tree canopies.

First published in 2013 by
wild dog
54A Alexandra Parade
Clifton Hill Vic 3068
Australia
+61 3 9419 9406
dog@wdog.com.au
wdog.com.au

Printed and bound in China by Everbest Printing Co Ltd

Distributed in the U.S.A. by
Scholastic Inc.
New York, NY 10012

ISBN: 978-174203550-5 (pbk)

5 4 3 2 1   13 14 15 16 17

PHOTO CREDITS:
All images courtesy of Shutterstock.
Green Python courtesy of Damian Goodall.

wild dog books would like to thank Dr Carla Litchfield
for her factual check of this book.

Glossary:

Camouflage: an animal's natural color or form that allows it to blend in with its surroundings.

Predator: an animal that hunts and eats other animals.

Prey: an animal that is hunted or eaten by another animal.

Index:

Tropical rainforests of the world:

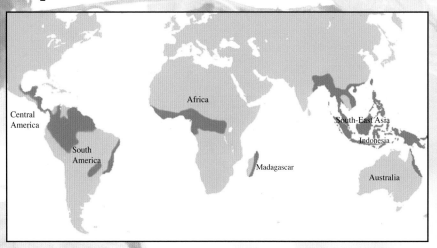

Central America, South America, Africa, Madagascar, South-East Asia, Indonesia, Australia